Jack

Enjoy!

Thea Johnson

THE HITLER I KNEW

A Young Girl's Memoirs of WW II in Germany

by

Thea Johnson

Bloomington, IN Milton Keynes, UK

authorHOUSE®

AuthorHouse™
1663 Liberty Drive, Suite 200
Bloomington, IN 47403
www.authorhouse.com
Phone: 1-800-839-8640

AuthorHouse™ UK Ltd.
500 Avebury Boulevard
Central Milton Keynes, MK9 2BE
www.authorhouse.co.uk
Phone: 08001974150

First published by AuthorHouse   10/3/2006

ISBN: 1-4259-5545-2 (sc)

Library of Congress Control Number: 2006908211

Printed in the United States of America
Bloomington, Indiana

This book is printed on acid-free paper.

The unique aspect of the title photo and the rest of Hitler's photos were from coupons that were attached to cigarette boxes that I collected during the war. (Zigaretten Bilderdienst). When I had enough coupons, I sent for photos of Hitler or other interesting photos during the Hitler era.

Some photos of the destruction of Ludwigshafen were sent to me in a booklet "Ludwigshafen in Trümmer" by Karl Mott, (wich are in the Stadtarchiv Ludwigshafen,) with compliments from Ludwigshafen's Lord Mayor (Oberbürgermeister) Ludwig for a Christmas present. The photos of the rebuilt Ludwigshafen are from postcards.

The combat photos used are with permission of the 100th Infantry Division Association. You may check their website at WWW.100thWW2.org

Die einmalige Erscheinung des Titelfotos and den Rest von Hitler's Fotos, waren von Zigarettenkupons, die ich waehrend des Krieges gesammelt hatte. Als ich genug Kupons hatte, schickte ich sie fuer Fotos von Hitler oder auch andere Fotos von Hitlers Zeitaler ein.

Manche Fotos von der Zerstörung von Ludwigshafen, wurden mir in einer Broschüre "Ludwigshafen in Trümmer", von Karl Mott, (die sich jetzt im Stadtarchiv Ludwigshafen befinden) mit Grüsse von Ludwigshafener Oberbürgermeister Ludwig, als Weihnachtsgeschenk geschickt. Die Fotos von dem Wiederaufbau von Ludwigshafen, sind von Ansichtskarten.

Die Kriegsbilder sind mit Erlaubnis von der 100th Infantry Division Association. Sie duerfen in ihre Webseite schauen: WWW.100thWW2. org

*I dedicate this book to my daughter Monika
and to my husband*

T.J.

ACKNOWLEDGEMENT

I would like to thank Ruth Donnocker and Brad Cummings for their dedication and time spent on helping me in proofreading my story. Also to Monika Slater and Gerald Chandler for scanning the photos, to Chuck Kovacs and to all my friends who encouraged me to write this story. A special thanks to my husband for his patience and to my German friends Renate Helbing and Hannes Arz, a special thank you for the help you gave me with the translation.

Thea Johnson 2006

TABLE OF CONTENTS

LIST OF PHOTOS

Book One

Chapter One

A City in Ruins

CHAPTER ONE
A CITY IN RUINS

When the war started in 1939, I was only nine years old and too young to know what it was all about. My hometown, Ludwigshafen, Germany, was a large industrial city. My father was Chief of Police and my mother was a nurse. My sister, Inge, was five years older than I. Everything seemed to be normal. We went to school, we went to church and sometimes we would go to see a Shirley Temple movie. Life seemed to be perfect as I could see it. In school the main topic was about "Adolf Hitler and the Third Reich." His sayings were mentioned in every class. His doctrines were our most important study.

One year Adolf Hitler visited our city. It was so exciting to see him in person; it was a big holiday and the whole city was out to greet him. It was such an honor to our city and people would talk about it for months.

In 1941 membership in the Hitler Youth had been made compulsory. All ten-year old boys and girls had to join the Jungvolk or Jungmaedelbund, the junior branches of the Hitler Youth. When I was ten years old, I joined the Hitler Youth. I was very excited about it. Every child wanted to belong to the Hitler Youth. We worshipped him and listened to many of his speeches. At one of our annual sports fests, he honored us with a special address to the Hitler Youth: "Hitler Youth, you are my youth," he said affectionately. "I believe in you and I claim you, for you are the Germany of tomorrow". Young voices responded the way we all felt, "Sieg Heil! Heil Hitler!" With the national anthem, we all stood with outstretched arms to join in.

I was so proud to wear my uniform; I looked forward to the meetings where we would learn how to do handicrafts, make little things out of wood to give children for Christmas presents, and learn about our leader, Adolf Hitler. Yes, we wanted to belong to him, to make him proud of his "Youth". Our Hitler Youth leaders demanded obedience and strict self-discipline and they were understanding and fair. We learned marching songs and I felt so proud when we marched and sang our songs. We worked hard to get ready for our yearly sports fest, where we all would compete and the best athletes would be honored with a medal. On Hitler's birthday, April 20, we always had a day off from school.

His frequent speeches never ceased to inspire me. The war would soon end in certain victory. There were daily radio announcements of victory from every fighting front. Hitler's bright red flags with the white circle and the black swastika waved from every great building.

German Hitler Youth 1942

Adolf Hitler in Garmisch

Hitler and his faithful supporters

Hitler always surrounded by Children

All the young men were called to bear arms. This pattern was followed of young men having to go to war. My father had served several years during World War I in France where he was wounded and shipped to England as a prisoner of war.

Our teacher suggested writing letters to an "unnamed soldier". The mail to the fighting forces had to be marked "Feldpost" and did not require postage. This was a great idea and almost everybody was writing to one Unknown Soldier. My girlfriend and I were so excited to think that we could bring a little sunshine to a soldier. I liked letters and I enjoyed writing. Sometimes a letter would come back with the stamp "Died for the Fuehrer and Fatherland" or "Missing at the Russian Front." How those few words would blow out the light in our hearts. In the early part of September 1939, we received notice that my first cousin was killed while fighting in Poland. I felt so bad about that.

My dad as Chief of Police tried to keep everything in law and order, but it became quite difficult. One night on his way home he encountered a group of men who were smashing windows and throwing furniture into the street. The house belonged to a Jewish family. A woman with her child ran to my father and begged him to stop the men from destroying her property. Although he wanted desperately to help the woman, my father was unable to. If he had interfered, the mob would have lynched him. Many more incidents happened with the Jewish people, but I never realized this until much later. I noticed that some people wore a yellow star with the inscription "Jude" on their clothing. I did not know anyone personally that wore a yellow star.

In early 1943 we started to have a few air raid alarms during the night. Mom and I would go to the balcony and watch with anticipation and wondered what would happen. We listened for the sound of airplanes. When they came, it was like watching a movie to see the airplanes in the searchlights. We would anxiously watch the first planes, the pathfinder squadron that marked the area with different colored marker flares to pinpoint the targets, descended slowly through the night sky on small parachutes. Their twinkling reds, greens and yellows were called "Christmas-trees" in German, an illusion given by the RAF's used to confuse the German radar systems. This was done to light up the whole town at night, in order for the rest of the bombers to drop their bombs accurately. During the day the children collected the aluminum strips and fragments of anti-aircraft shells. Boys, who traded them for play-cards, particularly prized those splinters.

After a few air raids, we decided that we should go to the basement just to be safe. There was a big bomb shelter 100 yards from our house. It was a great windowless fortress with concrete walls four meters thick and five stories high. It did get hit by bombs a couple of times, but it would only take a small piece of concrete out of the bunker. At times we would go across the street to that bomb shelter after the air raid alarm sounded. The children usually played cards or other little games, and after the all-clear signal we would go home and go to bed. Sometimes we would sit in the bomb shelter for hours and nothing happened. In our school the children were put through civil defense drills, complete with gasmasks. I hated those gasmasks; whenever I tried mine on, it gave me the feeling that I would suffocate.

I remember the first major bombing attack on our city. August 9, 1943 was a beautiful summer day, but all the bad news from the front, the daily increase of fallen soldiers and the increased bomb attacks on German cities made the people of Ludwigshafen uneasy and alarmed. The mood was not good; you just could not help but think that Ludwigshafen would be next; that thought alone was terrifying.

I was awakened from a deep sleep by the terrifying sound of the town's air raid alarm and the thunder of the approaching bombers. We could sense by the roaring of the approaching machines that this time they came in a much bigger number. As my parents, sister and I ran towards the safety of the cellar, all I had time to do was get a coat to wear over my pajamas. The house was shaking and parts of the ceiling began to fall. Bombs were falling all around our house. As we all huddled together in a corner of the cellar, we feared that each falling bomb would hit our house, when with a terrifying bang the lights went out. We sat in the dark under appalling bursts of explosions and awaited our end. I was truly frightened. The next moment there was someone kicking at the cellar door shouting, "Everybody out, the house is on fire!"

We ran to the street only to be caught in a blazing inferno. All around us burning wood and bricks were tumbling from our apartment house, while the bombs continued to fall. Ashes were falling down on me, my eyes were burning and I was unable to see where I was. There was nowhere to run, nowhere to hide. The whole city was burning. This bombardment seemed to go on forever. The night sky was red from fires and the air filled with smoke, it was a nightmare! How could anyone survive a bombing like that? I know that God saved me from certain death. I thought of the many lives that had been snuffed out. This bomb attack of August 9, 1943 was the first air raid on our city, with a long line of attacks that would follow. Who would have known that this was the beginning of destruction and death to our city?

After the bombardment we went to our church, which had a large basement with enough beds for each family that had lost their home. We stayed there until morning and went back to the house to see if we could salvage anything at all, but everything was completely destroyed. We had nothing left, just the clothes we wore that night. To be bombed out came so sudden and unexpected! We could have taken some of our belongings to the cellar, but we did not think that a bomb would hit our house.

I needed clothes, since I only had a coat on top of my pajamas. Mom always seemed to be able to find what we needed. She found a new place for us to move to and her sister gave us some clothes, pots and pans and a couple of chairs, just enough to start out with.

A destroyed apartment house

In 1943 when my sister turned 18, she was put on an anti-aircraft searchlight position, on the outskirts of town. It took my breath away. I was convinced that this was not right to put a girl in a position where she would have to man a searchlight or to shoot at the enemy airplanes while they were bombing our city.

We were all upset, even Inge, who could hardly wait to belong to the BDM (Bund Deutscher Maedels) "Circle of German Girls" and had high hopes to do something worthwhile, but not that. Especially not since we had attacks every day and to man the searchlights while bombs were falling was just impossible. She tried to do this job, but after a few terrifying incidents she came home and told us that she ran away. She could not do this. We immediately sent her to Bavaria to be with her aunt. A couple of days later, there were two men in civilian clothes, asking for my sister. That really scared me, but Mom told them that we had no idea where she was. We hoped that they would not find her.

My sister and I in 1947

With the appointment of Air Marshall Arthur Harris to Commander of the British Air Force, the air attacks became more intense and ruthless by bombing houses, churches, hospitals, historical buildings and monuments. "Bomber Harry" was hoping that the bombing of the cities would demoralize the population and thus weaken the morale of the German soldiers.

The Ludwigshafen police report of August 13, 1943 told of the horrific bombings. They reported the following statistic: "457 British bombers dropped 25,000 stick firebombs, 3,540 phosphor bombs, 129 high explosive bombs, 11 blockbusters and 24 canisters with phosphoric acid." All these were dropped in one night. 15,000 people were left homeless, approximately 900 houses were totaled and 1,800 were damaged. Three German Chemical Plants at Leuna, Ludwigshafen and Zeitz were the targets of a total of 146,000 British and American bombs.

On September 5 of the same year, 605 bombers left their deadly mark over the city and on September 23, there were 628 bombers. Beginning in December 1943, the American pilots assisted the British squadrons with their attacks. The people remained calm, even though their suffering was so great. What we did not know was that it would get even worse.

The bombings went on; there never seemed to be a pause. We were so exhausted. We hardly ate, never had a chance to take a bath or shower and were afraid to go to sleep. It seemed like the minute we closed our eyes, there either was the loud air raid alarm or we would wake up in the middle of a bombing. We did not bother to undress any more.

Thousands of people were killed in my hometown. I remember the solemn mass funerals. A bulldozer dug up large spaces in the cemetery. They were filled with many, many caskets. The people around sang the German National Anthem and then the caskets were covered with dirt.

The few hours we had without bombing we helped people who were trapped in buildings or picked up bricks and rubble and tried to clear the streets so traffic could pass. We put out fires together, forming spontaneous human chains to pass buckets of water from hand to hand. Neighbors relied on each other to guard their property and possessions. There were only women, children and old men left to do this; the young men were away fighting the war.

I went to the hospital a few times to visit my mother who was a nurse there. She tended to the Polish prisoners of war. The sight of the hospital grounds after an air raid haunted me for a long time. It was like a battlefield, the wounded sprawled on the lawns and doctors operating on them there. The Polish POW camp was located one mile past our house and the prisoners were marched by the house every morning to go to their workplace. Whenever there was an air raid and bombing, they were not allowed in a bomb-shelter. Several of those prisoners were killed or maimed from the falling bombs and where sent to the hospital.

Sometimes I would not go to the cellar when there was an air raid alarm. My girlfriend and I would stay in the kitchen and listened to the radio. When no one was around, we would tune in to BBC, the British Broadcasting station, and listen to the news. One-day dad came to the kitchen and caught us. He was very angry. "I never want to catch you girls listening to that station again. I will not go to the concentration camp for you."

We had to be very careful of what we did or what we said. Anyone who did not like you might tell the Gestapo that you had said something against the Fuehrer. They would come and take you away and most likely you would wind up in a concentration camp. Whenever I went into a store, I greeted every one with the important, "Heil Hitler," not with good morning.

To keep one's job one had to become a member of the Nazi Party. Because my father did not believe in the party, he refused to join. Subsequently he lost his job. He and some other men were picked up and loaded on a truck bound for the French border, where they were forced to help build the Siegfried Line to impede the movement of American tanks. We did not see my Father again until after the war.

I remember the arguments between my mother and father. Mom was all for joining the Nazi Party, but my father was not. She would tell him how much better it would be for us if he would join, but dad refused. He just could not be talked into something that he did not agree with.

Mom and Dad in 1942

In an effort to bridge the gulf between home and front, German radio stations transmitted family greetings to the men in programs like "Gruesse aus der Heimat" (greetings from home); also the Sunday musical requests dedicated to loved ones with the "Wunschkonzert". Everyone seemed to love this program; the people needed cheering up.

Within one month after we moved into our new apartment a bomb also hit that house. Luckily we were in a bomb shelter on the other side of the street. The house was completely destroyed. I could see the big crater in the cellar where the bomb exploded. Surprisingly, two people were in the basement, but got out alive by climbing through an opening that connected one house to the other. (Every apartment house in the block had to make an opening in the basement that connected it to the next apartment house, a hole big enough for a person to climb through.) It was strange, but I began to feel resigned to the idea of dying under a bomb. I was physically paralyzed with fright and with every air raid, this fear seemed to increase.

Once again we were left with nothing but our lives. We found another place in a house that had been hit by a bomb, but luckily half of the house could be lived in. By now, we did not care if we had to sleep on the floor; we just needed a place where we could be inside and not on the street.

Phone lines were cut, streetcars stopped running, the whole inner city was said to be a heap of rubble. The next night was just as bad, everything was destroyed, my school also burned down; I could not go there any more. The fire brigade and army units tried to cope with the enormous numbers of bombed out families who had nowhere to go; the municipal authorities erected temporary shelters in the city's outer suburbs.

The government made special quotas of brandy and real coffee beans available to bombed areas. I remember mom getting a bottle of champagne and while she opened it, the air-raid alarm started to blare. She poured the champagne into a bowl and gave my girlfriend and me a cup so we could drink it in a hurry, before the bombers came. I had no idea that it was alcohol. I don't remember if we became tipsy, I just knew that we did not want to waste it and drank a cupful and hurried to the bomb shelter.

We missed a lot of school when the bombings went on and so many people were killed. By Government order, many schools were evacuated to the countryside. Kinderlandverschickung or KLV as it became universally known. The children were to be sent away from the "areas threatened by air attack". Hitler had entrusted Baldur Von Schirach with the task of drawing up the guidelines and organizing the KLV. My class was sent to Bad Bergzabern. There we had plenty to eat, had school again and our Fuehrerin leaders made sure that we kept up with our way of staying fit and saw to it that we honored Hitler at all times.

KLV Lager Bad Bergzabern

I shared a room with seven girls and we became fast friends. One became my best friend. She shared her dresses with me, as I had practically nothing to wear since we were bombed out. Every morning after breakfast we had to go outdoors to salute the flag, and then we all marched to school. In the afternoon we marched back to our quarters, where we had our dinner and then did our homework; our leaders would also come to chat and teach us more about Adolf Hitler.

I am standing on the left, with my friends

I had been there for six months when my mother came to get me. It was getting so bad in the city, but she wanted me to be with her, no matter what might happen. It took us a long time to get back to town. The train would go for several miles then stop. We had to get off, because the railroad tracks were destroyed. At that moment there was another air-raid alarm and we could hear the droning noise of the approaching bombers. We were out in the open, just standing there, watching the sky filled with planes; we knew they were bombing Ludwigshafen again.

We could see the bombs raining down. I had never observed an air attack from far away; this time I could see it all. The earth literally shook from the explosions. I was shaking so much; I thought I would get sick. We had to walk along torn-up, mangled tracks and across gaping holes to get into another train that took us to the outskirts of town. We encountered a couple duds, which were big bombs that for some reason had not exploded when they hit the ground. They looked like torpedoes, approximately eight feet long with a 12-inch diameter. Those were called "Blockbusters" as they could destroy a whole block.

I tried to find some of my school friends, but all I could see were bombed out buildings. The town was totally destroyed. I found out that a phosphor bomb had killed my math teacher and his family. It was so sad. I wondered where all my friends were if they were still alive. It was amazing to see people still walking around on the streets when there were no houses left standing. They came out of the rubble and some made their homes in basements or bomb shelters. I saw a stovepipe sticking out of the ground with a sloping path down through the earth to the entrance of the cellar, where people lived, as best as they could.

The bombings continued non-stop. The British RAF came during the day and the American USAF came during the night to drop their bombs on us. We had only one thought, if only it would stop! But it did not stop. We thought in a moment our nerves would crack; although we wanted to cry out, we were not allowed to. We had to keep our composure. We were not allowed to be weak, because that is what we learned in the Hitler Youth. It was during the last phase of the war that the bombing became most severe and the loss of human life greatest.

Most of the people had left Ludwigshafen, most likely to the country where no bombs were dropped. Ludwigshafen had one of Germany's prize chemical producing centers, the IG Farben (BASF) where they produced products, which were of primary concern to the Wehrmacht.

IG produced all of Germany's synthetic rubber, lubricating oil, part of its synthetic gasoline, the greatest bulk of German explosives. IG played a big part in developing chemical warfare. They produced the poison gases for Germany and developed the most deadly gas Tabun. There was also the highway to France, where reinforcements for out troops would come. For these reasons demolishing our town was top priority.

On the roofs of the factory were anti-aircraft and searchlights to shoot down the attacking bombers. The Flak (anti-aircraft) was able to shoot down several of the bombers over our city. A few times I saw a German soldier with an American or British airman who had come down with a parachute, taking them somewhere to prison.

IG Farben (BASF) in rubble

At the end of the war the BASF factory area was a desolate stretch of ruins. The years of reconstruction between 1945 and 1948 were certainly the hardest in the hundred year's history of BASF. By 1978 BASF had become the largest chemical complex in Europe. It employs over 50,000 workers.

IG Farben (BASF) destroyed

The laboratory of IG Farben before and after an air raid

Bismarkstrasse after an air raid

A bombed out building in Ludwigstrasse

Friedenskirche (Church of Peace)

The Luther Church was destroyed but the tower remained

Bombed out buildings in Prinzregentenstrasse

By now we could hear the artillery. It was getting closer every day. We knew that the American troops were not far away. Conflicts between German and American troops would be inevitable. So as not to be caught in the middle of combat, we began to think of a means of escape. There was a notice that the Rhine Bridge would be blown up the next morning, delaying the American troops from crossing the Rhine. Despite the certain approach of the Americans, we were still getting daily radio announcements that the war would soon end in certain victory.

My mother decided that this was the time for us to escape, to go to Bavaria where she had two sisters. We left the same evening. There were hundreds of people at the train station. We waited and waited. More people came, but no train. We waited all night. I was so cold and tired and wanted to go back home. Shortly before noon the next day there was a loud blast. The bridge had been destroyed. We could never go back.

The Rhine Bridge the Germans blew up

Some time in the afternoon the train finally arrived. Everyone pushed and shoved trying to get into the train. The doors were not enough, so they climbed through the windows. Boxes and suitcases were thrown in. We were very lucky to get inside. If it were not for two men who helped us climb through a window, we would have never made it. Finally the train pulled away from the station, leaving many people behind.

We had been riding about one hour when the train stopped in the middle of nowhere. Small enemy airplanes were approaching our train and started to shoot at us. We, along with others, jumped off the train and ran into the nearby woods. The planes made several attacks and came down so close we could see the pilots. After all was quiet, we returned to the train and started on our way again. The atmosphere on the train was very tense. Everyone watched the sky for enemy planes. Sure enough, someone shouted, "Here they come again! Why doesn't he stop that train?"

The train went faster and faster. It seemed like it was out of control. The airplanes swooped down on us and were shooting, but the train never slowed down. A few more seconds and the brakes came on so hard, we fell from our seats — we were safe inside a tunnel! We stayed there until after dark, when it was safe for the train to go on without being attacked.

Finally we reached Bavaria where the signs of war did not exist. There were no air raids, there was plenty of food, sleep at night came easily and I could take a bath again. It was like paradise.

On July 20, 1944 we heard on the news about an assassination attempt on Hitler. Count von Stauffenberg, who wanted to oust the Nazi regime and end World War II, led the attempt. The conspirators placed a bomb in a briefcase that was left under a desk where Hitler was holding a meeting. The bomb exploded, but Hitler emerged unhurt. Stauffenberg and the other officers involved in the plot were sentenced to death and hanged at the Gestapo offices in Berlin. Other civilians involved in the attempt escaped.

While we were enjoying our stay in Bavaria, there were vicious fights between the American and German troops around Ludwigshafen. The Americans were trying to get across the Rhine River with a lot of difficulties, since the Germans had blown up the Rhine Bridge.

Infantrymen of the 399ᵗʰ Infantry Regiment advance aboard an M4A4
Sherman tank near Ludwigshafen

24 March 1945: Infantrymen of Item Company/399th Infantry Regiment advance aboard an M4A4 Sherman tank near Ludwigshafen, Germany. After the massive Seventh Army breakthrough of the brittle German defenses in the Palatinate which began on 15 March (Operation UNDERTONE), speed was of the essence if German forces were to be denied the opportunity to reorganize and make another stand. Whenever possible, the infantry advanced mounted on whatever was available, whether tanks, trucks, or even captured enemy vehicles.

Infantry advances through the rubble of Ludwigshafen

25 March 1945: An infantry squad advances through the rubbled remains of the city of Ludwigshafen, Germany. At the moment this photo was taken, all organized resistance had ceased, but snipers were still active in some of the burned-out buildings, and mortar and artillery fire was still arriving from German units near Mannheim, on the other side of the Rhine River.

❖ Rhine Crossing
Ludwigshafen—Mannheim
31 March 1945

Rhine crossing Ludwigshafen-Mannheim 31 March 1945

31ˢᵗ Engineer Combat Battalion emplaces a bridge

Early April 1945: Combat engineers of the 31st Engineer Combat Battalion emplace a bridge. German artillery — particularly "flak" or antiaircraft artillery units played havoc with the engineers' attempts to emplace a bridge. Frequently, no sooner would a bridge be completed and the first tanks roll on when the Germans would destroy the span, sending the vehicles and their crews to the bottom of the river. Until the American armor got across the river, the infantrymen of the 100th Infantry Division were at the mercy of German armor (including several heavy *Jagdpanther* tank destroyers) prowling the rubbled streets.

Even though it was not officially announced, the whole country whispered that Adolph Hitler along with Eva Braun committed suicide. His friend, Propaganda Minister Joseph Goebels and his wife poisoned their five children then ordered an SS attendant to shoot him and his wife. I was stunned, I could not entertain the thought that Hitler, my idol, took the coward's way out. What was going to happen now!

CHAPTER TWO

A CITY AND LIFE REBUILT

Admiral Doenitz

In May 1945 Admiral Doenitz spoke over the radio, telling us, by Hitler's last will that he was now the new leader of the nation. He announced the total surrender of Germany to the Allies. My stupefied mind refused to believe it. Many Germans did what I contemplated; they followed Hitler to the bitter end and committed suicide. People could not imagine any future after Germany's defeat. Other Nazis did not have to take their own lives; some one else did the job for them. Admiral Doeniz was our leader for only 24 hours.

When we received word that the Americans had crossed the Rhine and were pressing on towards Bavaria, panic struck everywhere. My aunt, with whom I was staying, wanted to cut her wrist and mine, anything rather than fall into the hands of the enemy. We were afraid what they might do to us, but I was young and determined not to give up my life so easily.

One night I was awakened by a rather strange noise. Looking out the window I saw an eerie sight – German soldiers by the hundreds were retreating from the war zone. It was dark outside and it looked like a column of ghosts. They did not make any noise, they just shuffled along. In the morning, more German soldiers passed; we went outside and gave them refreshments. They told us that they did not want to fight any more. The SS (Hitler's elite troops) had picked up several German soldiers who refused to go on and fight; the SS hung their bodies on light poles as a warning for the rest of the German troops.

I spent a lot of time outdoors to make sure that when a German soldier came by I was ready to give him refreshment. One time right after I gave a soldier a glass of water, a tank drove up and stopped. I stood there and smiled, ready to offer a glass of water when I realized that was a different looking uniform and that soldier spoke to me with a heavy accent. I was paralyzed with fright, afraid to run away. I thought they might shoot me. Then my mother came to the door, screaming: "Get in here, those are the Americans!" and I ran into the house.

When the Americans came, not a shot was fired. The village had white flags in almost every window and the German soldiers surrendered. The Americans took over all the important places. The German civilian men were picked up and taken to the city for questioning. The soldiers became prisoners of war.

It was a tragedy that families had to face; many would have to wait years for the status of their men listed as missing to be clarified. Families pinned pictures of captured or missing soldiers to notice boards of railway stations in the hope that a returning soldier might bring them news. In the war over 5,000,000 German soldiers died, at least one million German civilians were killed and over 400,000 were a result of bombings

We stayed in Bavaria for one year. Everything was nice and pleasant. One time I took my bicycle and rode to town to see what was going on. The Americans were all over town with their jeeps, trucks and tanks; some were handing out chocolate and gum to the children. I encountered several men who escaped the concentration camp; they were still wearing their striped clothing. One came over to me and tried to take my bicycle, but I did a lot of screaming. An American soldier came to see what was going on and helped me to keep my bike. He told me to go home. It was not safe to be there.

Some of the villagers were ordered to take a tour of the concentration camp in Dachau. The Americans wanted the German people to see what atrocities had been inflicted. No one could ever imagine the horror. How could this happen without people knowing what was going on?

Mom decided to go back home to Ludwigshafen, which was now under French occupation. Since it was so soon after the war there were no passenger trains. For two days we traveled on flat bed railroad cars to get to Ludwigshafen. There were many people who were doing the same as we were. We waited for hours until a train came. We climbed on board and hoped that the train would take us as close as possible to where we wanted to go. It was so cold and windy sitting on top of the coal car. After hours of slow traveling, the train stopped and we had to get off and wait for another train that would take us towards home. We sat by the railroad tracks for many hours and waited. Finally a train came and stopped, we climbed on board and hoped that it would take us closer to home. We had traveled for two days and had not eaten; I was so hungry and so cold.

After many, many hours we finally made it. We were surprised and very happy to see that Dad was alive. We found him at the old house, which was 75% destroyed, but he had made himself a little place where he could live. He told us, when the American forces advanced towards the French and German border, everyone left the Siegfried Line and tried to make it back home. After he was home again, he could hear the continuous firing of guns all around him. When he was in the apartment, he had to duck a couple of times, because he was afraid one of the bullets or cannons would hit the house, which it did, right above the kitchen window, when he was making himself a sandwich.

The battle between the Germans and the Americans was fierce and Ludwigshafen was right in the middle of it. Dad stayed in the house and hoped that whatever would happen, he would leave it up to the Lord. In the middle of all that shooting, one American soldier came in the house and checked the apartment. He opened a suitcase and Dad told me that he was really worried, because he had a Mauser (pistol) in his suitcase. When the soldier discovered the pistol, he grabbed it, put it inside his jacket and never said a word. Then another soldier came into the apartment, pulled a mattress out of the bed and took it to the basement to sleep. After a few hours he came back, brought the mattress back and gave my father a present, a small inkwell inscribed with "Souvenir from New York". This was a very unusual and pleasant surprise.

We encountered several differences between the French zone and the American zone. There was an enforced curfew in the French zone-no one was allowed on the streets after 7 PM. The Rhine Bridge was the link between the French and the American zones. No one was allowed to go across without a pass.

Food was scarce in the French zone. The farmers were the only ones who had plenty of everything. My sister and I went out of town to the farmers and begged from door to door for just one potato, bread or vegetable. Without silver, gold or linens to give in return for food, doors were slammed in our faces. Before going home we sneaked into a farmer's field and helped ourselves to a bag full of vegetables, so as not to return home empty-handed. The hunger that followed German defeat was the most common pain during and after the war. If there were any food to be found, we would take it to survive.

One day I decided that I would go over to the American zone where I had an aunt, but without a pass, they would not let me go across. When I saw a truck, which had to stop, approach the bridge, I asked if I could ride in the back of the truck just to get across. Without a problem I was on the other side. I went to visit my aunt and in the evening, I was on my way back home. This time I had to go through two guards. The first one was an American soldier; he let me go without a problem. When I reached the French side, it was different. That French soldier made such a fuss because I did not have a pass and he took me to the guardhouse where he threatened me with jail.

After a couple of hours an officer came in and he was just as bad. He yelled at me, "My hand in your face if you are lying," and I sat there several more hours crying, having to listen to him screaming at me. After a while he asked me how old I was and when I told him that I was 15, he yelled at the soldiers and then told me, "Get out, go home!" I was petrified! I was afraid that he would shoot me in the back. When I was far enough away, I ran all the way home.

Some of the French soldiers did not treat the German people nicely at all; some were downright nasty. Maybe they hated us because we won the war with France and the Germans occupied their country. Now they were taking it out on us. They put signs on the streetcars that the German people were not allowed to enter in the front; we had to enter in the back and stay in the back. When a German man tried to get in the front, a French soldier pistol-whipped him and the man fell to the ground.

The French took away railroad cars full of flour, coal and whatever they wanted, and sent them to France, while most of the German people in the French zone were starving. We would get only one loaf of bread a week and a little milk and rice, no potatoes and no vegetables. We were happy when we were able to get sour milk and lentils that were full of bugs. Mom would make fun of it and told us not to complain because we are getting meat with our soup.

Once a week we went to the butcher to collect a can full of water with a little fat in it. Mother could make the best soup out of it. I was totally undernourished; my mother took me to the doctor and insisted that I should get a double ration-card, which was great, since I did not eat more; it just gave my family a little more to eat. Once in a while mom would get up at four o'clock in the morning to stand in line for horsemeat.

We could get double the portion of horsemeat with our ration cards. Most of the time there was not enough meat at the butcher shop, so Mom had to try again the following week.

We finally were able to get a pass, so we could go across the Rhine Bridge into the American zone, where we had relatives who had a small farm. They were happy to see us and we were invited to stay for dinner. Afterward, they gave us a loaf of bread to take home with us. When we reached the bridge, the Americans checked our pockets and one wanted to see what I held in my arms. It was the loaf of bread and he took it away from me. I felt terrible and I cried, but he did not give it back to me. I am sure he did not need it; he just wanted to be mean. On the other side of the bridge, the French soldiers also checked our pockets, but we had nothing they were interested in.

When winter came there was no coal or wood with which to heat the apartment. The water froze in the pipes and we had to wear our coats, mittens and scarves in the apartment to keep warm. Every evening after dark, my sister and I sneaked out to the railroad tracks about a half-mile away. There was a steep grade where all the trains heading for France had to slow down. People from the neighborhood were there every night. The men would climb up onto the railcar and throw coal down. We would follow with our bags and pick it up. When we had our bags full, we went home and enjoyed a few hours in a warm kitchen.

At another time someone broke open a railcar loaded with flour and people filled their bags with flour instead of coal. One night when we were busy picking up coal, I looked up to see a giant of a French policeman pointing a pistol at us. I dropped my bag and ran over the railroad tracks into the darkness. I never went to the tracks at night again.

My sister became very ill, she coughed a lot and when we took her to the hospital, they discovered that she had TB. She was sent to a sanatorium somewhere in the country for a couple of months. I also had to be checked for TB, but I was all right.

School started again. We had to complete two grades in one year to make up for the year we had lost during the war. The big problem was that most of the schools were destroyed and the few that were not destroyed had to double up, with half of the pupils going from 8 to12 PM and the other half from 1 to 5 PM. The school was so cold and our teacher asked us to bring one piece of firewood to school every day, so we could warm our room and we would be able to write and do our homework. The winter had been the harshest anyone could remember and shortage of food became chronic, leading to further ration cuts. Children collapsed from hunger in the classrooms.

One day mom met one of the Polish prisoners of war that she took care of in the hospital. He invited us to his wedding. What a celebration! There was so much food, I had not seen in a lifetime. We ate as much as we could, but afterward we got so very sick. We were not used to that good and rich food and our stomachs could not take it.

Winter finally ended and the weather began to get warmer. The American people must have heard of our plight in Ludwigshafen, for a group of American Quakers arrived and remained for almost two years. Once a week every citizen of Ludwigshafen received a supply of oatmeal, margarine and peanut butter. We also received clothing from the USA. The Quakers organized groups of Germans to clean up the city. On weekends the teenagers met with them to learn American songs and about America.

Life began to improve a little. The Rhine Bridge was opened so we could travel to the American zone and food was easier to get. Many years would be required to restore Ludwigshafen but the people of the city, myself included, once again had a future to look forward to.

There was so much destroyed and Ludwigshafen did not have enough money or people to do the rebuilding. They hired "Guest Workers" from other countries, mainly from Italy, to help with the re-construction. It took years to clear out the rubble, heavy equipment was brought in and the destroyed buildings were removed. It was a lot of work and it would take many years to rebuild our city. Displaced people from Ludwigshafen started to come back, but there was no place for them. The Mayor tried to discourage them since they would not be able to find housing.

The Ludwigshafen police offered my father his old job in the police department back, but he declined; instead he was involved with the task of writing a column for the sports section and being in charge of the police sports department.

My sister married a German soldier that had returned from Siberia, serving five years as a prisoner of war. Many of the German soldiers died there of starvation or they froze to death. He came back with a lot of health problems. He was plagued with chronic bronchitis and asthma and died after a few years.

I finished school and found a job working for the American Government as an office clerk in Mannheim, which was in the American zone. My friends envied me because the pay was a lot better than what a German firm could offer. While working there, I met an American soldier that was stationed there.

It was rather difficult to go out with an American soldier so soon after the war. The German men I worked with did not like it, but after dating my friend for a while, the Germans became reconciled to it. There was so much more to do in the American Zone. We would go to the American movie and afterwards to the snack bar, where I could eat anything I wanted and as much as I wanted. Some days the American soldiers marched through town and it was always great to see them looking so clean and sharp.

I wanted to introduce my friend to my parents, but even the Americans needed a pass to enter the French zone. After a one-year courtship, we were engaged and one year later we married. I left my hometown to continue my life in the USA. I will never forget the day I left my home. Mom and dad took me to the train station and dad sobbed so hard, his heart was broken. He told me that he would rather have me dead so he could visit me at the cemetery and put flowers on my grave, instead of me going to America where he might never see me again. He died in 1955.

My husband and I when we first met

I return to my hometown every year to visit my family and friends and sometimes I take a bus tour with my girlfriend. On one of those tours I met a lady on the bus and we stayed together while the tour-guide showed us the sights. On the third day the lady asked me what my maiden name was. When I told her, she screamed and carried on and I wondered what happened. She told me that we went to school together and to the KLV Lager and we shared the same room at that time. That was 60 years ago. She told me that she always wondered what happened to me and thought about me often.

She was still in touch with some of the other school-buddies from 1943 and they get together at times. When they all heard about our surprised encounter, we all met and had a great time, before it was time for me to leave for the US. Since then, every year when I go to Germany, we all meet and make it a class reunion.

When I visit my hometown, I can see the improvements that were made. Ludwigshafen often looked like one huge building site. From the very beginning the principles underlying the overall building plan were characterized by a degree of far-sightedness. The city fathers have made full use of this unique opportunity of rebuilding an almost completely destroyed city. Extensive parks and greens fill the spaces between the individual communities. Bypasses, through streets and roads help to keep the center of the city free from all unnecessary traffic.

Ludwigshafen, the city along the Rhine River, despite its industrial complexes, huge concerns and worldwide chemical enterprises, has now become a city in which it is worth living.

The new train station

The new road towards the Rhine Bridge

A new departmentstore

Overview of Ludwigshafen and Rhine with Mannheim

Bismarkstrasse

Ludwigshafen on the Rhine at night

EPILOGUE

I wanted to write this story to show how blindly we followed a leader that promised a great future for Germany. He would not let anyone or anything stop him from invading other countries and killing millions of innocent people. He had taken the best of Germany and corrupted it with his evil purposes. He took the loyalty of the German people and led them into endless, hopeless wars. He took the bravery of the youth and commanded them to die.

As a Hitler Youth I believed that I was part of something that was noble and good and patriotic. When I began hearing about the Nuremberg War Trial, I was very confused about my heroic national leaders. Men like Admiral Doenitz, Chief of the Submarine Command; Erich Reader, Commander in Chief of the German Navy, Alfred Jodl, Chief of Staff of the High Command, and Baldur Von Schirach, our Youth Leader had been our heroes- it was very disturbing. I did not understand how these men had ravaged my country with their ideologies and barbarous acts.

The trial was held at Nuremberg. Here then, between November 20, 1945, and October 1, 1946, the trial of the major war criminals took place. Twenty-four men who were considered war criminals were selected for trial before the international tribunal consisting of the representatives of the four victorious powers: America, Britain, France, and Russia.

The sentences were announced on October 1, 1946. It was a terrible tragedy and though I myself did not think that all of the twelve men deserved hanging, and the years of imprisonment were rather high, the world calls it "Justice" so who am I to question it. "The victor will always be the judge, and the vanquished always the accused."

I very much wished that I had thought differently at the time of war, that I had seen through this disastrous regime and waged resistance against it; of course I was much to young to do anything about it. The greatest achievement was to have survived and I thank God that he stood by me and saved me.

He who dwells in the shelter of the Most High
Will rest in the shadow of the Almighty.
I will say of the Lord, "He is my refuge and
My Fortress, my God, in whom I trust."
Surely he will save you from the fowler's snare
And from the deadly pestilence.
He will cover you with his feathers,
And under his wings you will find refuge;
His faithfulness will be your shield and rampart. (Psalm 91:1-4)

Surely it was by God's grace that I survived this war and now make my home in the U.S. where we are free to worship God. We were not allowed to read or own a Bible during Hitler's time. Now I own a Bible and I have accepted Jesus into my heart. I have recognized the fact that I am a sinner and have accepted Christ's sacrifice on the cross as payment for the death penalty of my sin before a perfect and holy God.

Because I've accepted the resurrected Christ as my personal Savior, I know that I will spend eternity in his awesome presence just as my hometown of Ludwigshafen has been made new, Christ has renewed my life and given me an eternal hope and joy which no person or circumstance can extinguish. He will also renew you and become the light onto your path if you will accept him as your savior today.

"Therefore if any man be in Christ, he is a new creature:
The old has gone, the new has come." (II Corinthians 5:17)

To order additional copies of

THE HITLER I KNEW

Call 888-280-7715

Or please visit our web site at
www.authorhouse.com

Also available at:
www.amazon.com
and
www.google.com

Zweites Buch

In deutscher Verfassung

So wie ich Hitler sah

So erlebte ich als junges Mädchen
die Hitlerzeit

*Für meine Tochter Monika
und meinen Mann*

T.J.

DANKSAGUNG

An dieser Stelle möchte ich mich bei allen ganz herzlich bedanken, besonders bei Ruth Donnocker und Brad Cummings für das hingebungsvolle Korrekturlesen, auch Monika Slater für das skandieren der Fotos, Chuck Kovacs und an alle meine Freunde die mich ermutigten diese Biographie zu schreiben. Auch einen besonderen Dank an meinen Mann für seine Geduld während ich dies schrieb und ein ganz besonderes Dankeschön an Renate Helbing und Hannes Arz die mir mit der Übersetzung halfen.

Thea Johnson 2006

TABLE OF CONTENTS

LIST OF FOTOS

ZWEITES BUCH

ERSTER TEIL

EINE STADT IN RUINEN

ERSTER TEIL
EINE STADT IN RUINEN

Als der Krieg 1939 begann, war ich neun Jahre alt und zu jung, um die Bedeutung zu erfassen. Meine Heimatstadt Ludwigshafen war eine große Industriestadt. Mein Vater war Polizeiinspektor und meine Mutter arbeitete als Krankenschwester. Meine Schwester Inge war fünf Jahre älter als ich. Alles war normal. Wir gingen zur Schule, in die Kirche und manches Mal in das Kino um Shirley Temple zu sehen. Für mich war das Leben in Ordnung. In der Schule lernten wir beeindruckt die Geschichte über „Adolf Hitler und das Dritte Reich". Seine Reden wurden in jeder Klasse besprochen. Seine Grundsätze waren sehr bedeutende Lehren für uns.

Einmal besuchte er sogar unsere Stadt. Das war ein großes Ereignis ihn persönlich zu sehen. Es war ein Feiertag und die ganze Stadt war auf den Beinen ihn zu begrüßen. Das war ein Jubel und geschrei! Es war eine große Ehre für unsere Stadt und jeder sprach lange darüber.

Im Jahr 1941 wurde die Mitgliedschaft zur Hitler Jugend Pflicht. Als ich zehn Jahre alt war, wurde ich Mitglied. Ich war ganz begeistert, jedes Kind wollte zur Hitlerjugend gehören. Wir verehrten ihn und hörten viele seiner Ansprachen.

An einem von unseren jährlichen Sportfesten hat er uns mit einer speziellen Ansprache an die Hitler Jugend geehrt: „Hitlerjugend, ihr seid meine Jugend"sagte er herzlich." Ich glaube an euch und ich ermutige euch, denn ihr seid das Deutschland von morgen". Junge Stimmen erwiderten mit Gefühl "Sieg Heil! Heil Hitler!" Bei der Nationalhymne machten wir alle mit ausgestreckten Armen mit.

Ich war so stolz meine Uniform zu tragen; ich freute mich auf die Treffen zum Basteln wo wir kleine Dinge als Weihnachtsgeschenke für Kinder herzustellen lernten und über unseren Führer Adolf Hitler unterrichtet wurden. Ja, wir wollten ihm folgen um ihn stolz auf „Seine Jugend „ machen.

Unsere Hitlerjugendführerinnen verlangten Gehorsam und strikte Disziplin, sie waren verständnisvoll und gerecht. Wir lernten Marschlieder und ich war so stolz wenn wir marschierten und unsere Lieder sangen. Wir trainierten sehr hart für unser jährliches Sportfest, wo wir alle teilnahmen und die besten Sportler mit einer Medaille ausgezeichnet wurden. Ganz besonders toll war es an Hitler's Geburtstag, den 20. April, da hatten wir immer schulfrei.

Seine häufigen Reden haben nie aufgehört mich zu beeindrucken. Der Krieg wird gewiss sehr bald mit einem Sieg beendet sein. Täglich kamen Radiomeldungen vom Sieg auf den Schlachtfeldern. Hitlers Hakenkreuzfahnen wehten von jedem großen Gebäude.

Deutsche Hitlerjugend 1942

Adolf Hitler in Garmisch

Hitler und seine treuen Anhänger

Hitler, von Kindern umgeben

Alle junge Männer wurden zu den Waffen gerufen. Dieser Ruf betrifft in jedem Krieg immer die junge Männer. Mein Vater wurde damals im ersten Weltkrieg in Frankreich als Soldat verwundet und wurde als Kriegsgefangener nach England geschickt.

Unsere Lehrerin schlug uns vor, an einen unbekannten Soldaten zu schreiben. Die Post zu den kämpfenden Truppen wurde als „Feldpost"bezeichnet und kostete kein Porto. Das war eine gute Idee und beinahe jeder schrieb an einen unbekannten Soldaten. Meine Freundin und ich waren ganz aufgeregt in dem Glauben, einem Soldaten etwas Sonnenschein zu bringen. Ich liebte es Briefe zu bekommen und ich freute mich, Briefe zu schreiben.

Manchmal kam ein Brief zurück mit dem Stempel: „Gestorben für Führer und Vaterland oder in Russland vermisst". Diese paar Worte trafen uns mitten in das Herz. Anfangs September 1939-bekamen auch wir die Nachricht, daß mein Cousin in Polen gefallen war. Es war sehr traurig.

Mein Vater, als Polizeiinspektor, versuchte Gesetz und Ordnung zu halten. Aber es gab Schwierigkeiten. Eines Abends, auf seinem Nachhauseweg stieß er mit einer Gruppe von Männern zusammen, die Fensterscheiben einwarfen und Möbel auf die Straße warfen. Das Haus gehörte einer jüdischen Familie. Eine Frau mit ihrem Kind rannte zu meinem Vater und bat ihn, die Männer von der Zerstörung abzuhalten. Er wollte der Frau helfen, doch es war unmöglich für ihn. Wenn er eingegriffen hätte, der Mob hätte ihn gelyncht. Erst später wurde mir klar, wie die Juden verfolgt wurden. Ich sah ein paar Leute die einen gelben Stern an ihrer Kleidung trugen, aber persönlich kannte ich niemand.

Anfang 1943 begann der Fliegeralarm in der Nacht. Mutti und ich gingen auf den Balkon und beobachteten mit Verwunderung das Ereignis. Wir hörten das Geräusch der Flugzeuge. Als sie kamen, war es wie im Film, so sahen wir die Flugzeuge im Scheinwerferlicht. Das erste Flugzeug, warf etwas ab, das in allen Farben glitzerte, in rot, grün und gelb, welches aussah wie ein Weihnachtsbaum. Das war um das deutsche Radarsystem durcheinander zu bringen und um die ganze Stadt in der Nacht zu erleuchten, damit der Rest von den Bombern ihr Ziel genau treffen konnten. Am Tag suchten die Kinder nach Bombensplitter, besonders die Jungen, die tauschten die größten Splitter für Spielkarten.

Nach ein paar Luftangriffen hatten wir uns entschlossen in den Keller zu gehen um sicherer zu sein. Es gab einen großen Luftschutzbunker etwa 100 Meter von unserem Haus. Er sah aus wie ein großer Zementklotz, fünf Stockwerke hoch. Er wurde ein paar Mal getroffen, aber es war nur ein unwesentliches Stück davon weg gesprengt. Manchmal gingen wir über die Straße zu dem Bunker, nachdem die Sirene Luftschutzalarm gegeben hatte. Die Kinder spielten Karten oder andere Spiele und nach der Entwarnung gingen wir nach hause und zu Bett. Manchesmal saßen wir für Stunden im Luftschutzkeller und nichts passierte. In der Schule hatten wir fast täglich defence drill mit Gasmasken. Ich haßte meine Gasmaske, jedes mal wenn ich sie anzog gab es mir das Gefühl als ob ich ersticken müßte.

Ich erinnere mich an den ersten gewaltigen Bombenangriff in unserer Stadt. Der 9. August 1943 war ein wunderschöner Sommertag aber schlechte Nachrichten von der Front und die Liste der gefallenen Soldaten nahm täglich zu. Die täglichen Bombenangriffe auf deutsche Städte beunruhigten und alarmierten die Bevölkerung von Ludwigshafen. Die Stimmung war nicht gut. Man konnte nichts tun, und man glaubte, dass Ludwigshafen als nächstes dran kam. Der Gedanke daran war schrecklich.

Ich erwachte aus einem tiefen Schlaf von einer Sirene direkt neben unserem Haus und dem Donner der ankommenden Bomber. Wir konnten am röhrenden Ton der Maschinen fühlen, dass es dieses mal ein größerer Angriff war. Als meine Eltern, meine Schwester und ich in den sicheren Keller rannten, hatte ich nur noch Zeit, meinen Mantel über meinen Schlafanzug anzuziehen.

Das Haus hat gewackelt und Stücke von der Decke fielen herab. Bomben fielen rund um unser Haus. Wir drückten uns zusammen in eine Ecke im Keller vor Angst, dass eine Bombe unser Haus treffen könnte. Mit einem Knall ging das Licht aus. Wir saßen im Dunkeln mit dem entsetzlichen Krach der Explosionen und erwarteten unser Ende. Ich hatte entsetzliche Angst Im nächsten Moment kam jemand und schrie: „ Alles raus, das Haus brennt."

Wir rannten auf die Straße, wo uns ein flammendes Inferno empfing. Überall brannte Holz und flogen Steine von unseren Haus durch die Luft, während die Bomben unaufhörlich fielen. Es regnete Asche auf mich, meine Augen brannten, es war mir nicht möglich, zu sehen wo ich war. Es gab nichts wohin wir rennen, nichts wo wir uns verstecken konnten. Die ganze Stadt brannte. Der Bombenangriff schien nie vorüber zu gehen.

Der nächtliche Himmel war rot vom Feuer und die Luft gefüllt mit Rauch. Es war ein Albtraum. Wie konnte nur jemand solch einen Bombenangriff überleben? Gott beschützte mich vom sicheren Tot. Ich dachte an die vielen Leben, die ausgelöscht wurden. Dieser Bombenangriff vom 9. August 1943 war der erste Luftangriff auf unsere Stadt, dem noch eine große Anzahl folgen sollten. Wer hätte gedacht, dass dies der Beginn der Zerstörung und des Todes in unserer Stadt war?

Ein zerstörtes Wohnhaus

Im Jahr 1943 als meine Schwester 18 Jahre alt war, wurde sie zur Fliegerabwehr berufen. Ich war sprachlos, ich war überzeugt, daß so etwas nicht richtig war, ein Mädchen in solch eine Position zu schicken, um einen Scheinwerfer zu bedienen, der das Licht auf die feindliche Flugzeuge richtete oder sie gar abzuschießen, während sie unsere Stadt bombardierten.

Wir waren alle verwirrt, auch Inge, die kaum warten konnte zum BDM zu kommen und etwas ganz besonderes zu tun, aber nicht dieses. Besonders nicht bei den täglichen Bombenangriffen und dann noch den Scheinwerfer zu bedienen während die Bomben fielen. Sie versuchte diese Arbeit zu machen, aber nach ein paar schlimmen Erlebnissen, kam sie nach Hause und sagte uns, daß sie geflüchtet ist. Wir haben sie sofort nach Bayern zu ihrer Tante geschickt. Ein paar Tage später kamen zwei Männer in Zivil und haben nach meiner Schwester gefragt. Das hat uns wirklich schockiert. Aber Mutti sagte ihnen, dass sie keine Ahnung hat, wo sie ist. Wir hofften, dass die sie nicht finden würden.

Meine Schwester und ich im Jahr 1947

Mit der Ernennung von Luftmarschall Arthur Harris zum Kommandeur der britischen Luftwaffe wurden die Luftangriffe intensiver und rücksichtsloser. Es wurden Häuser, Kirchen, Krankenhäuser, historische Gebäude und Denkmäler bombardiert. „Bomber Harry"hoffte, dass Bombenangriffe auf die Stadt die Bevölkerung demoralisieren würde und damit auch die Moral der deutschen Soldaten schwächen würde.

Der Ludwigshafener Polizeireport berichtet über ein entsetzliches Bombardement. Hier ist die Statistik: "457 britische Bomber warfen 25.000 Brandbomben ab, 3.540 Phosphorbomben und 24 Kanister mit Phosphorsäure". Dies alles in einer Nacht. 15.000 Menschen wurden heimatlos, ungefähr 900 Häuser wurden zerstört und 1.800 beschädigt. Drei deutsche Chemiefabriken in Leuna, Ludwigshafen und Zeitz waren das Ziel der 146.000 britischen und amerikanischen Bomben.

Am 5. September im selben Jahr trafen 605 Bomber ihr tödliches Ziel über der Stadt und am 23. September waren es 628 Bomber. Anfang Dezember 1943 halfen die amerikanischen Piloten den britischen Geschwadern bei ihren Angriffen. Die Bevölkerung verhielt sich ruhig, obwohl die Angst sehr groß war. Was wir nicht wussten, war, dass es noch schlimmer werden sollte.

Nach dem Bombenangriff gingen wir zur Kirche, welche ein großes Kellergeschoss mit genug Betten für jede Familie besaß, die ihr Heim verloren hatte. Wir blieben bis zum Morgen dort und gingen dann zu unserem Haus zurück um nachzusehen ob noch etwas zu retten sei, doch es war alles zerstört. Wir hatten nichts, nur die Kleider, die wir nachts getragen hatten. Das Ausgebombtsein kam so plötzlich und unerwartet, wir hätten einige unserer Habseligkeiten mit in den Keller nehmen können, aber wir dachten nicht daran, dass eine Bombe unser Haus treffen könnte.

Ich brauchte Kleider, weil ich nur einen Mantel über dem Schlafanzug trug. Mutti machte es immer möglich etwas zu organisieren. Sie fand einen neuen Ort, wo wir wohnen konnten und ihre Schwester gab uns einige Kleider, Töpfe und Pfannen und ein paar Stühle, gerade genug um neu zu beginnen.

Die Angriffe dauerten an, es schien ohne Pause. Wir waren erschöpft. Wir aßen kaum, hatten keine Möglichkeit zu baden oder duschen und fürchteten uns, schlafen zu gehen. Es kam uns vor, wenn wir nur eine Minute die Augen zu machten, wir würden entweder von der lauten Luftschutzsirene oder mitten in einem Bombenangriff aufgeweckt. Wir trauten uns nicht mehr, uns auszuziehen.

Tausende Menschen starben in meiner Heimatstadt. Ich erinnere mich an eine feierliche Massenbeerdigung. Ein Bagger hob eine große Grube im Friedhof aus. Sie wurde mit vielen, vielen Särgen gefüllt. Die Leute sangen die deutsche Nationalhymne und dann wurden die Särge mit Erde bedeckt. In den wenigen Stunden ohne Bombenangriffe, halfen wir den Leuten, die in den Gebäuden eingeschlossen waren, räumten Steine und Schutt weg und versuchten die Straßen sauber zu machen, damit der Verkehr durch kam. Es waren nur Frauen, Kinder und alte Männer die diese Arbeit machten, die jungen Männer waren weg der Front.

Öfter besuchte ich meine Mutter im Krankenhaus, wo sie als Krankenschwester arbeitete. Sie war in der Abteilung wo verwundete polnische Kriegsgefangene waren. Der Anblick im Hospital nach einem Luftangriff schockte mich noch lange Zeit. Es war wie auf einem Schlachtfeld, die Verwundeten lagen in den Gängen und die Ärzte operierten sie dort.

Das polnische Kriegsgefangenenlager war einen Kilometer von unserem Haus entfernt und jeden morgen marschierten sie an unserem Haus vorbei, zu ihren Arbeitsplätzen. Bei einem Bombenangriff durften sie nicht in unseren Bunker. Ein paar Gefangene wurden dadurch getötet oder verwundet, und wurden in das Krankenhaus gebracht.

Einmal wollte ich bei einem Luftalarm nicht in den Keller gehen. Meine Freundin und ich, wir blieben in der Küche und hörten Radio. Wenn keiner da war, stellten wir BBC ein und hörten Nachrichten. Eines Tages kam mein Vater in die Küche und überraschte uns. Er war sehr ärgerlich. „Ich will euch Mädchen nie mehr erwischen wenn ihr diesen Sender hört; ich will nicht ins Konzentrationslager kommen wegen euch".

Wir mussten sehr vorsichtig sein, was wir taten und sagten. Jemand, der dich nicht mochte, könnte der Gestapo mitteilen, dass du etwas gegen den Führer gesagt hast. Dann kommen sie, nehmen dich mit, meistens verschwindest du im Konzentrationslager. Wir wussten alle vom Konzentrationslager, aber nicht was es alles schlimmes dort gab. Jedes mal wenn ich in einen Laden ging, grüßte ich jeden mit dem besagten „Heil Hitler"nicht mit „Guten Morgen", man bestand darauf.

Um seine Stellung zu behalten, musste man Mitglied der Nazi Partei sein. Mein Vater war nicht in der Partei, er lehnte diese Verbindung ab. Deswegen verlor er seine Arbeit. Er und einige andere Männer wurden abgeholt und auf einen Lastwagen geladen und an die französische Grenze befördert, wo sie gezwungen wurden an der Siegfried Linie zu arbeiten um die amerikanischen Truppen aufzuhalten. Wir sahen meinen Vater nicht mehr bis der Krieg zu Ende war.

Ich erinnere mich an die Auseinandersetzungen zwischen meiner Mutter und meinem Vater. Meine Mutter wollte unbedingt in die Nazipartei eintreten, aber mein Vater wollte nicht. Sie erklärte ihm, wie viel besser es für uns wäre, wenn er mitmachen würde, aber er weigerte sich. Man konnte ihn nicht überreden etwas zu tun, mit dem er nicht einverstanden war.

Mutter und Vater 1942

Mit einem Versuch die Entfernung der Heimat und Front zu überbrücken, übertrug der deutsche Rundfunk Grüße von Familien zu den Männer an der Front mit Programmen wie „Grüße aus der Heimat"und an jedem Sonntag brachten sie ein musikalisches Program „Wunschkonzert", womit jede Familie mit einem schönen Lied den Geliebten grüßen ließ.

Innerhalb eines Monats nach dem wir in eine neue Wohnung eingezogen waren, zerstörte eine Bombe auch dieses Haus. Zum Glück waren wir im Luftschutzbunker auf der anderen Straßenseite. Das Haus war vollständig zerstört. Ich konnte einen großen Krater im Keller sehen, wo die Bombe explodiert war.

Überraschenderweise, waren zwei Leute in diesem Untergeschoss und sie kamen lebend davon, da sie durch eine Öffnung im Keller in das andere Haus klettern konnten. (Jedes Wohnhaus musste in den Kellern eine Öffnung frei machen, damit man durch das nächste Haus entkommen konnte). Seltsam, ich fand mich mit dem Gedanken ab, dass ich im Bombenhagel umkomme, doch ich war bei jedem Luftangriff wie gelähmt vor Angst und es wurde immer schlimmer.

Wieder einmal hatten wir nichts als unser Leben. Wir fanden wieder eine andere Unterkunft, doch diese war halb zerstört. Wir konnten trotzdem darin wohnen. Nun, es war uns egal, ob wir auf dem Boden schliefen, Hauptsache wir hatten ein Dach über dem Kopf und waren nicht auf der Straße.

Telefonkabel waren zerstört, Straßenbahnen konnten nicht mehr fahren, die ganze Innenstadt war vollständig in Schutt. Die nächste Nacht war genau so schlimm, alles wurde zerstört, sogar meine Schule brannte nieder; ich konnte nicht mehr in die Schule gehen.

Es fiel viel Schulunterricht während der Bombenangriffe aus und viele Leute wurden getötet. Es wurde von der Regierung verordnet, dass die Schulen auf das Land umgesiedelt würden, zur Kinderlandverschickung. Baldur Von Schirach wurde mit diesen Pläne von Hitler angefordert. Meine Klasse wurde nach Bad Bergzabern geschickt. Dort hatten wir viel zu essen, auch Unterricht, und unsere Führerinnen sorgten dafür, dass wir sportlich fit blieben und Hitler weiterhin verehrten.

I Kinderlandverschickung in Bad Bergzabern

Ich bin die erste von links mit meinen
Freundinnen

Ich teilte mit sieben Mädchen ein Zimmer und wir wurden schnell Freunde. Eine wurde meine beste Freundin. Sie teilte ihre Kleidung mit mir, weil ich nichts anzuziehen hatte, da wir ausgebombt waren. Jeden Morgen nach dem Frühstück gingen wir ins Freie um die Fahne zu grüßen, erst dann marschierten wir zur Schule. Am Nachmittag kamen wir zurück in unsere Unterkunft, dort hatten wir Abendessen und machten unsere Hausaufgaben. Unsere Führerinnen waren da um uns zu beaufsichtigen und uns mehr über Hitler zu erzählen.

Nachdem ich sechs Monate dort war, kam meine Mutter um mich abzuholen. Es war so schlimm in der Stadt, aber sie wolle mich bei sich haben, egal was passierte. Es dauerte sehr lange in die Stadt zu kommen. Der Zug fuhr etliche Kilometer, dann war Halt. Wir mussten aussteigen weil die Schienen zerstört waren.

In diesem Moment war wieder ein Fliegeralarm und wir konnten den dröhnenden Lärm der sich nähernden Bomber hören. Wir standen draußen und sahen den Himmel voller Flugzeuge. Wir wussten, dass sie Ludwigshafen wieder angriffen. Wir konnten den Bombenregen fallen sehen. Ich hatte noch nie einen Bombenangriff von weiter weg beobachtet, dieses mal konnte ich es sehen. Es war so aufregend.

Die Erde bebte von den Explosionen. Mir wurde so schlecht und ich konnte nicht aufhören zu zittern. Wir mussten entlang der vollkommen zerstörten Schienen und über offene Löcher steigen um in einen anderen Zug zu kommen, der uns an den Rand der Stadt brachte. Warum konnte ich nicht im Lager bleiben wo es ruhig war? Ich haße diese Bomardierungen!

Wir entdeckten einige Blindgänger, das sind große Bomben die aus irgend einem Grund nicht explodierten als sie auf den Boden fielen. Sie sahen aus wie Torpedos: ungefähr 3 Meter lang und 30 cm Durchmesser. Wir sagten "Blockbusters" weil sie einen ganzen Wohnblock vernichten konnten.

Ich versuchte, meine Schulfreundinnen zu finden, doch alle Gebäude waren ausgebombt. Die Stadt war vollständig zerstört. Ich hatte herausgefunden, daß mein Lehrer und seine Familie durch eine Phosphorbombe umgekommen waren. Das war sehr traurig.

Ich wollte gerne wissen, wo meine Freundinnen waren, ob sie noch lebten. Es war erstaunlich, die Leute auf der Straße zu sehen, wo doch kein Haus mehr stand. Sie kamen aus den Trümmern und die meisten lebten dort in den Kellern oder in den Bunkern. Ich sah ein Ofenrohr aus dem Grund stecken, das nach unten zu einer Kellertühr führte, wo Leute wohnten, so gut es ging.

Die Bombenangriffe kamen ohne Unterbrechung. Die britische RAF kam tagsüber und die amerikanische USAF während der Nacht, um ihre Bomben abzuwerfen. Man hatte nur einen Gedanken, wann ist endlich Schluss. Aber es hörte nicht auf. Die Nerven waren dem Zerreißen nahe - du wolltest schreien - doch es war nicht erlaubt, - du musstest Ruhe bewahren - es war nicht erlaubt schwach zu werden, so hatten wir es bei der Hitlerjugend gelernt. Es war in der letzten Phase des Krieges, wo die Bombardierung so schrecklich und der Verlust von Menschen das Schlimmste war.

Die meisten Leute hatten Ludwigshafen verlassen. Meistens auf das Land, wo keine Bomben fielen. Ludwigshafen hatte eins von Deutschlands berühmtesten Chemiefabriken, IG Farben (BASF); die Produktion war in erster Linie für die Wehrmacht bestimmt.

IG stellte alles von Deutschlands synthetischem Gummi, Schmieröl und einen Teil des synthetischen Benzins her, die größte Masse von Deutschlands Sprengstoff, Plastik und Leichtmetall. IG spielte eine große Rolle in der Entwicklung von Chemiegas für die Kriegsführung. IG produzierte Giftgase für Deutschland und das tödlichste Gas Tabun. Tabun ist ein Nervengift, tödlich und schnell wirksam. Ludwigshafen war auch die Hauptverkehrsstraße nach Frankreich, für den Nachschub für unsere Truppen. Aus diesem Grund wurde unsere Stadt hauptsächlich zerstört.

IG Farben (BASF) in Trümmern

Auf den Dächern der Fabrik waren die Luftabwehr und Scheinwerfer positioniert um die angreifenden Bomber abzuschießen. Der Flak (Luftabwehr) war es möglich, einige der Bomber abzuschießen, über unserer Stadt. Einige Male sah ich einen deutschen Soldaten, der einen amerikanischen oder britischen Piloten, der mit einem Fallschirm absprang, gefangen nahm .

Am Ende des Krieges blieb von der Industrie BASF nur noch ein trostloses, weites Ruinenfeld übrig. Alle Betriebe waren stillgelegt. Das ganze Gebiet war bedeckt mit Schutt. Die Jahre des Wiederaufbaus zwischen 1945 und 1948 waren sicherlich die härtesten in der hundertjährigen Geschichte der BASF. Im Jahre 1978 wurde die BASF der größte Chemiekonzern in Europa, und beschäftigte über 50.000 Mitarbeiter.

IG Farben (BASF) zerstört

Das Labor der IG Farben vor und nach
den Luftangriffen

Bismarckstraße nach einem Luftangriff

Ein ausgebombtes Haus in der Ludwigstrasse

Friedenskirche

Die Lutherkirche wurde zerstört, aber der Kirchturm blieb stehen.

Ausgebombtes Haus in der Prinzregentenstraße

Ganz nahe konnten wir die Artillerie hören. Sie kam täglich näher. Wir wussten, dass die amerikanischen Truppen nicht weit weg waren. Zusammenstöße zwischen deutschen und amerikanischen Truppen waren unvermeidlich. Um nicht mitten im Kriegsgeschehen gefangen zu werden, begannen wir an einen Weg zum Entkommen zu suchen. Dann gab es eine Ankündigung, daß am nächsten Morgen die Rheinbrücke in die Luft gesprengt würde, damit das Überqueren des Rheins für die amerikanischen Truppen verzögert würde. Trotz dem sicheren Nahen der Amerikaner, bekamen wir immer noch die Radioansagen, dass der Krieg bald siegreich zu Ende ginge.

Meine Mutter beschloss, dass es Zeit war zu flüchten, nach Bayern zu gehen, wo sie zwei Schwestern hatte. Am gleichen Abend gingen wir los. Es waren hunderte von Leuten auf dem Bahnhof. Wir warteten und warteten. Es kamen immer mehr Leute, aber kein Zug. Wir warteten die ganze Nacht. Mir war es kalt und ich war müde und wollte nach Hause gehen. Kurz vor Mittag des nächsten Tages gab es einen lauten Knall. Die Brücke war zerstört, wir konnten nicht zurück.

Die gesprengte Rheinbrücke

Irgendwann am Nachmittag kam endlich der Zug. Alles drückte und schob um in den Zug zu kommen. Es gab nicht genug Türen und so kletterten sie durch die Fenster. Kisten und Koffer wurden hineingeworfen. Wir waren heilfroh hineingekommen zu sein. Doch wenn uns nicht zwei Männer geholfen hätten, durch das Fenster zu klettern, wir hätten es nie geschafft. Endlich fuhr der Zug aus dem Bahnhof, viele Leute mussten zurück bleiben.

Wir waren schon über eine Stunde gefahren, als der Zug mitten auf der Strecke stoppte. Kleine, feindliche Flugzeuge kamen und näherten sich unserem Zug und begannen zu schießen. Wir und alle anderen, sprangen aus dem Zug und rannten in den nahen Wald. Die Flugzeuge machten einige Angriffe und kamen so nahe, dass wir sogar die Piloten sehen konnten. Als alles ruhig war, kehrten wir zum Zug zurück und fuhren weiter. Die Stimmung im Zug war sehr gedrückt. Jeder hielt am Himmel nach herannahenden Flugzeugen Ausschau. Plötzlich schrie jemand: „ Sie sind wieder da! Warum hält der Zug nicht?"

Der Zug wurde schneller und schneller. Es schien als wäre er außer Kontrolle. Die Flugzeuge stießen herab und schossen, aber der Zug fuhr nicht langsamer. Ein paar Sekunden später wurde hart gebremst, wir fielen von den Sitzen - wir waren in einem Tunnel in Sicherheit! Wir blieben bis zur Dunkelheit dort, das war sicherer für den Zug ohne Angriff weiterzufahren.

Endlich erreichten wir Bayern, wo es keine Anzeichen des Krieges gab. Es gab dort keine Luftangriffe, reichlich Lebensmittel, nachts durchzuschlafen war kein Problem, und wir konnten wieder baden. Es war wie im Paradies.

Am 20. Juli 1944 hörten wir im Radio, dass ein Attentatsversuch auf Hitler gemacht wurde. Graf von Stauffenberg, der die Nazi Regierung weg schaffen wollte und damit den Weltkrieg beenden wollte, war der Anführer. Er hatte eine Bombe in seiner Aktentasche und tat sie unter den Tisch, wo Hitler eine Konferenz hielt. Die Bombe explodierte, aber Hitler kam heil davon. Stauffenberg und die anderen Offiziere die in dem Plan verwickelt waren, wurden zum Tode verurteilt und bei der Gestapo in Berlin gehängt. Andere Zivilisten die auch darin verwickelt waren sind entkommen.

Während wir froh waren, in Bayern zu sein, gab es brutale Kämpfe zwischen amerikanischen und deutschen Truppen in Ludwigshafen. Die Amerikaner versuchten mit großen Schwierigkeiten den Rhein zu überqueren, da die Deutschen die Rheinbrücke gesprengt hatten.

Soldaten vom 399th Infanterie Regiment auf einem M4A4 Sherman Panzer in der Nähe von Ludwigshafen

24. März 1945: Mit der Operation UNDERTONE, die am 15. März begann, gelang der 7. Armee der Durchbruch durch die geschwächten deutschen linien. Geschwindigkeit war von da an wichhtig, um den deutschen Verteidigern die Möglichkeit zu nehmen sich wieder zu organisieren und in Stellung zu gehen. Die Infanterie nahm dabei von allem Besitz um den Vormarsch nicht aufzuhalten, egal ob Panzer, Lastwagen oder sogar erbeutete feindliche Fahrzeuge.

Infanterie beim Vormarsch durch die Ruinen von Ludwigshafen

25. März 1945: Eine Infanteriegruppe beim Vormarsch durch die Ruinen von Ludwigshafen, Germany. Als dieses Foto aufgenommen wurde, war der ganze organisierte Wiederstand gebrochen, aber Heckenschützen waren noch in den ausgebombten Gebäuden, und deutsche Einheiten, auf der anderen Seite des Rheinufers, in der Naehe von Mannheim, nahmen die Infanterie mit Granaten und Artillerie unter Beschuss.

Rheinüberquerung Mannheim-Ludwigshafen

31ˢᵗ Enginieur Kampfbattalion bauen eine Brücke

Anfang Appril 1945: Einsatzingenieure von der 31. Enginieurkampfgruppe bauen eine Brücke. Deutsche Artillerie – hauptsächlich "Flak" oder Fliegerabwehr-einheit, versuchten Chaos zu verursachen. Kaum war eine Brücke fertig und der erste Panzer auf dem Weg, zerstörten die Deutschen die Brücke und die Fahrzeuge mit Besatzung stürzten in den Fluß. Bis die amerikanische Panzer über den Fluß kamen, war die 100. Infanterie Division deutschen Truppen in den zertrümmerten Straßen ausgesetzt.

Wenn es auch nicht öffentlich bekannt gegeben wurde, das ganze Land flüsterte, dass Adolf Hitler mit Eva Braun Selbstmord begangen hätte. Sein Propagandaminister Josef Göbbels und seine Frau vergifteten ihre fünf Kinder und befahlen der SS ihn und seine Frau zu erschießen. Ich war geschockt. Ich konnte den Gedanken nicht fassen, daß Hitler, mein Idol, diesen feigen Weg wählte, was sollte nun geschehen?

Zweiter Teil

Eine Stadt und Leben
beim Aufbau

Admiral Dönitz

Im Mai 1945 sprach Admiral Doenitz zu uns im Radio, er verkündete Hitler's letzten Willen. Er war nun der Führer der Nation. Er verkündete die totale Kapitulation von Deutschland an die Alliierten. Er war Deutschland's Führer für 24 Stunden. Ich war so blöd, es nicht zu glauben. Viele Deutsche erwägten Hitler bis zum bitteren Ende zu folgen und Selbstmord zu begehen. Andere Nazis nahmen sich nicht ihr Leben, andere taten diesen Job für sie.

Als wir hörten, dass die Amerikaner den Rhein überquert hatten und nun Richtung Bayern vorstießen, ergriff jeden Panik. Meine Tante, bei der wir wohnten, wollte sich die Pulsadern aufschneiden und meinte, alles sei besser als in die Hände des Feindes zu fallen. Wir fürchteten uns davor, was sie mit uns machen würden, doch ich war jung und entschlossen, mein Leben nicht so leicht zu opfern.

Eines Nachts wachte ich von einem komischen Geräusch auf. Als ich aus dem Fenster schaute, sah ich deutsche Soldaten, hunderte, die von der Front zurück kamen. Es war dunkel draußen und alles sah wie ein Geisterzug aus. Sie machten kein Geräusch, sie schlurften vorbei. Am Morgen kamen noch mehr deutsche Soldaten vorbei. Wir gingen hinaus und gaben ihnen Erfrischungen. Sie sagten daß sie nicht mehr länger kämpfen wollten. Die SS (Hitler's Elitetruppe) nahm jeden deutschen Soldaten gefangen, der sich weigerte zu kämpfen, hängte ihn an öffentlichen Schauplätzen auf, als Warnung für den Rest der deutschen Truppen

Ich verbrachte viel Zeit im Freien, um auch gewiß keinen deutschen Soldaten zu verpassen um ihm Erfrischungen zu geben. Gerade als ich einem Soldaten ein Glas Wasser reichte, kam ein Panzer vorbei und stoppte. Ich stand da und lächelte, bereit auch ein Glas Wasser anzubieten, als ich wahrnahm, daß es eine unterschiedliche Uniform war und der Soldat zu mir in einen harten Akzent sprach. Ich war gelähmt vor Schreck, fürchtete, wenn ich wegrennen würde, sie würden auf mich schießen. Dann kam meine Mutter an die Tür und schrie: "Komm herein, das sind die Amerikaner!" und ich rannte in das Haus.

Als die Amerikaner kamen, fiel kein Schuß. Der Ort hatte weiße Flaggen in beinahe jedem Fenster und die deutschen Soldaten eingeschlossen. Die Amerikaner übernahmen alle bedeutenden Einrichtungen. Die männlichen Zivilisten wurden abgeholt und zum Verhör in die Stadt gebracht. Die Soldaten kamen in Kriegsgefangenschaft.

Es war eine traurige Angelegenheit für manche Familien. Sie mußten Jahre warten, before sie erfuhren ob ihre Männer die vermißt waren, noch am Leben sind. Sie klebten Bilder von vermißten Soldaten an Bahnhoftafeln in der Hoffnung daß heimkehrende Soldaten ihnen gute Nachricht bringen. Im Krieg sind über 5,000,000 deutsche Soldaten gefallen, und zumindest eine million deutsche Zivilisten wurden getötet und über 400,000 als Folge von Bombenangriffen.

Wir blieben ein Jahr in Bayern. Alles war schön und erfreulich. Eines Tages nahm ich mein Fahrrad und fuhr in die Stadt, um zu sehen, was es dort gab. Die Amerikaner waren überall in der Stadt mit ihren Jeeps, Lastwagen und Panzern. Einige verteilten Schokolade und Kaugummi an die Kinder. Ich begegnete einigen Männern, die dem Konzentrationslager entkommen waren, sie trugen noch ihre gestreiften Kleider. Einer kam zu mir und versuchte, mir mein Fahrrad wegzunehmen, aber ich schrie fürchterlich. Ein amerikanischer Soldat kam um zu sehen was los war und er half mir das Rad zu behalten. Aber er empfahl mir, heim zu gehen. Es war nicht sicher dort.

Einige Leute aus dem Dorf wurden zu einer Reise nach Dachau in das Konzentrationslage gesandt; die Amerikaner wollten der deutschen Bevölkerung zeigen, was für grausames Leid dort geschehen war. Keiner konnte sich diesen Horror vorstellen. Wie konnte so etwas passieren, ohne daß das Volk etwas davon ahnte?

Mutter beschloß nach Ludwigshafen heimzukehren, das nun unter französischer Verwaltung stand. Da es bald nach Kriegsende war, gab es keine Personenzüge. Zwei Tage fuhren wir im Güterzug nach Ludwigshafen. Viele Leute machten es genau so. Wir warteten Stunden bis ein Zug kam. Wir kletterten hinauf und hofften, daß der Zug uns soweit wie möglich dort hinbrachte, wo wir hin wollten. Es war kalt und windig oben auf dem Kohlenwagen zu sitzen.

Nach Stunden langsamer Fahrt stoppte der Zug und wir mußten aussteigen und auf den nächsten Zug warten, der uns weiter Richtung Heimat brachte. Wir fuhren zwei Tage und hatten nichts zu essen, ich war so hungrig und mir war kalt.

Nach vielen, vielen Stunden waren wir endlich zu Hause. Wir waren überrascht und sehr glücklich, daß mein Vater am Leben war. Wir fanden ihn im alten Haus, das zu 75% zerstört war. Er hatte sich einen kleinen Platz zum wohnen eingerichtet. Papa erzählte uns, als die amerikanische Kampftruppen in die Nähe von der französichen und deutschen Grenze kamen, flüchteten alle Männer die an der Siegfried Linie gearbeitet hatten, und versuchten so schnell wie möglich nach

Hause zu kommen. Als er nach Hause kam, war ein unmöglicher Kampf zwischen den Amerikaner und den Deutschen, mit Kanonen und Gewehren. Papa versuchte von dem Fenster fern zu bleiben, weil er Angst hatte, daß eine Kanone das Haus treffen könnte, das tatsächlich der Fall war. Eine Kugel traf das Haus direkt über dem Küchenfenster, als Papa sich ein belegtes Brot machte.

Ganz plötzlich kam ein amerikanischer Soldat in die Wohnung und kontrollierte alles. Er durchwühlte einen Koffer und Papa erzählte mir, daß er ängstlich war, weil er in seinem Koffer eine Mauser (Pistole) hatte. Der Soldat entdeckte sie, ergriff sie blitzschnell und steckte sie in seine Jacke, ohne ein Wort zu sagen. Dann kam ein anderer Soldat, ging in das Schlazimmer und entfernte eine Matratze, nahm sie in den Keller zum schlafen. Nach ein paar Stunden kam er zurück und gab meinem Vater ein Geschenk, ein kleines Tintenfaß, mit der Inschrift "Andenken von New York."

Wir entdeckten einige Unterschiede zwischen der französischen und der amerikanischen Zone. Es bestand ein gesetzliches Ausgehverbot in der französischen Zone nach 7 Uhr abends auf den Straßen. Die Rheinbrücke war die Verbindung zwischen der französischen und der amerikanische Zone. Niemand war es erlaubt, ohne einen Paß hinüber zu gehen.

Die Lebensmittel waren in der französischen Zone knapp. Die Bauern waren die einzigen, die genug hatten. Meine Schwester und ich gingen auf das Land und bettelten von Tür zu Tür um einige Kartoffeln, etwas Brot oder Gemüse. Ohne Silber, Gold oder Wäsche gab es nichts gegen Lebensmittel zu tauschen, die Türen wurden uns vor der Nase zugeschlagen. Bevor wir heim gingen, schlichen wir auf die Felder der Bauern und füllten uns selbst die Tasche mit Gemüse, so daß wir nicht mit leeren Händen nach Hause kamen.

Eines Tages beschloß ich, hinüber in die amerikanische Zone zu meiner Tante zu gehen, aber ohne Paß würden sie mich nicht passieren lassen. Als ich einen Lastwagen sah, der sich der Brücke näherte und stoppen mußte, frug ich, ob ich auf dem Rücksitz mitfahren könnte. Ohne Problem war ich auf der anderen Seite. Ich besuchte meine Tante und am Abend machte ich mich auf den Weg nach Hause.

Dieses Mal hatte ich zwei Wachen zu passieren. Die erste war ein amerikanischer Soldat. Er ließ mich ohne Problem durch. Als ich auf die französische Seite kam, war es anderst. Der französische Soldat machte einen riesigen Wirbel, weil ich keinen Paß hatte, nahm mich mit zum Wachhäuschen, wo er mir mit Gefängnis drohte.

Nach einigen Stunden kam ein Offizier herein und er war genau so schlimm. Er brüllte mich an: „Ich schlage dir ins Gesicht, wenn du lügst", ich saß mehrere Stunden weinend dort und hörte ihn mit mir schreien. Nach einer Weile fragte er mich, wie alt ich sei und ich erwiderte, daß ich 15 sei. Er brüllte den Soldaten an und sagte dann zu mir „ hinaus, geh heim". Ich war wie versteinert! Ich fürchtete, daß man mir in der Rücken schießen würde. Als ich weit genug weg war, rannte ich den ganzen Weg nach Hause.

Einige französische Soldaten behandelten die Deutschen nicht freundlich, einige waren richtig ekelhaft. Vielleicht haßten sie uns, weil wir den Krieg gegen Frankreich gewonnen hatten und ihr Land eroberten. Nun zahlten sie es uns zurück. Sie schrieben an die Straßenbahnen, daß es den Deutschen nicht erlaubt ist, den vorderen Teil zu benutzen. Wir mußten hinten einsteigen und im Hinterteil bleiben. Als ein Deutscher Mann versuchte, vorne einzusteigen, schlug ein französischer Soldat ihn mit der Pistole zu Boden.

Die Franzosen beschlagnahmten waggonweise Mehl, Kohlen und alles was sie wollten und sandten es nach Frankreich, während die meisten Deutschen in der französischen Zone hungerten. Wir bekamen nur einen Laib Brot in der Woche und ein bischen Milch. Wir waren glücklich wenn wir saure Milch bekamen und Linsen, die voller Käfer waren. Mama machte sich einen Spaß daraus und sagte, daß wir uns nicht beschweren sollten, wir hätten schließlich Fleisch in unserer Suppe.

Einmal in der Woche konnten wir vom Metzger Fleischbrühe bekommen; Mutter konnte die beste Suppe daraus machen. Ich war total unterernährt und meine Mutter nahm mich zu unserem Hausarzt und er verschrieb mir, daß ich eine doppelte Rationskarte bekomme. So gab es ein bischen mehr Lebensmittel für die ganze Familie. Ab und zu stand meine Mutter schon morgens um vier Uhr auf und stellte sich beim Metzger in Schlange auf, der doppelte Portion Pferdefleisch per Rationskarte verkaufte. Manchesmal war es ganz schnell ausverkauft, und sie mußte es ein anderes Mal noch einmal versuchen.

Endlich erhielten wir einen Paß, so daß wir die Rheinbrücke überqueren und in die amerikanische Zone gehen konnten. Wir hatten dort Verwandte, die einen kleinen Bauernhof hatten. Sie freuten sich, uns zu sehen und luden uns zum Abendessen ein. Später gaben sie uns noch einen Laib Brot mit nach Hause.

Als wir über die Brücke gingen, kontrollierten die Amerikaner unsere Taschen und einer wollte wissen, was ich unter meinem Arm trug. Es war das Brot und er nahm es mir ab. Mir wurde ganz schlecht und ich weinte, aber er gab es mir nicht zurück. Ich war sicher daß er es nicht brauchte, er war nur gemein. Auf der anderen Seite der Brücke, machten die französischen Soldaten das gleiche, sie kontrollierten unsere Taschen, doch wir hatten nichts mehr darin, was sie interessierte.

Als es Winter wurde, hatten wir kaum Kohlen oder Holz um unsere Wohnung zu heizen. Das Wasser fror in den Leitungen und wir trugen Mäntel, Handschuhe und Schal in der Wohnung um uns warm zu halten. Jeden Abend, bei Dunkelheit, schlichen meine Schwester und ich hinaus zu der Eisenbahnstrecke über einen Kilometer weit weg. Dort war eine Steigung, bei der alle Eisenbahnwagen, die nach Frankreich bestimmt waren, langsam fahren mußten. Leute aus der Nachbarschaft waren jeden Abend dort. Die Männer kletterten in die Wagen und warfen die Kohlen hinunter. Wir folgten mit unseren Taschen und sammelten sie auf. Wenn unsere Taschen voll waren, gingen wir nach Hause und freuten uns auf einige Stunden in einer warmen Küche.

Ein anderes Mal brach jemand einen Eisenbahnwagen auf, der Mehl geladen hatte und die Leute füllten ihre Taschen mit Mehl anstatt mit Kohle. Eines abends, als wir mit Kohle aufsammeln beschäftigt waren, schaute ich auf und sah einen Hünen von einem französischen Polizisten, der mit der Pistole auf uns zeigte. Ich ließ meine Tasche fallen und rannte über die Eisenbahngleise in die Dunkelheit. Ich ging niemals mehr zu den Gleisen.

Meine Schwester wurde sehr krank, sie bekam einen Hustenanfall nach dem anderen. Als wir sie zum Arzt brachte, stellte sich heraus, dass sie TB hatte. Sie mußte für ein paar Monate in ein Sanatorium, irgendwo auf dem Land. Ich wurde auch untersucht, aber ich war gesund.

Die Schule begann wieder. Wir mußten in einem Jahr zwei Klassen durchlaufen, da wir während dem Krieg viel Zeit verloren hatten. Das größte Problem war, daß die meisten der Schulen zerstört waren und die wenigen, die nicht zerstört waren, mußten doppelt besetzt werden. Die eine Hälfte der Schüler ging morgens von 8- 12 Uhr und die andere Hälfte von 1- 5 Uhr nachmittags zum Unterricht.

Ich war glücklich meine Freunde wieder zu sehen. Das Schulzimmer war so kalt und unser Lehrer bat uns ein stück Holz von zu Hause mitzubringen, so daß unser Schulzimmer warm wurde und wir schreiben und unsere Hausaufgaben machen konnten. Der Winter war der schlimmste in langer Zeit und das andauernde knappe Essen wurde noch weniger. Kinder brachen vor Hunger in der Schule zusammen.

Eines Tages begegnete meine Mutter einem Polen, den sie damals im Krankenhaus als Kriegsgefangener pflegte. Er erkannte sie und lud uns zu seiner Hochzeit ein. Da gab es so viel leckeres zu essen, wir waren im siebten Himmel. Was es da zu Essen gab, hatten wir Jahre lang nicht gesehen. Das schlimme war, wir wurden von dem vielen guten Essen sehr krank; unser Magen konnte diese reichliche Nahrung nicht vertragen.

Endlich war der Winter zu Ende und es wurde wärmer. Das amerikanische Volk mußte von unserer Notlage in Ludwigshafen gehört haben. Eine Gruppe von amerikanischen Quakern kam und blieb beinahe zwei Jahre. Einmal in der Woche erhielt jeder Einwohner von Ludwigshafen eine Lieferung von Weizenmehl, Margarine und Erdnußbutter. Wir erhielten auch Kleidung aus den USA. Die Quaker organisierten Gruppen von Deutschen, die die Stadt reinigten. An den Wochenenden trafen sich die jungen Leute um amerikanische Lieder und alles über Amerika zu lernen.

Das Leben besserte sich ein wenig. Die Rheinbrücke war geöffnet und wir konnten in die amerikanische Zone fahren wo Lebensmittel leichter zu bekommen waren. Einige Jahre wird es benötigen, um Ludwigshafen wieder aufzubauen, aber das Volk in der Stadt, mich eingeschlossen, hatten allen Grund hoffnungsvoll in die Zukunft zu schauen.

Es war soviel zerstört und Ludwigshafen hatte nicht genug Geld oder Leute zum Wiederaufbau. Sie heuerten Gastarbeiter von anderen Ländern an, hauptsächlich aus Italien, um beim Wiederaufbau zu helfen. Es dauerte Jahre um die Trümmer wegzuräumen, schwere Ausrüstung wurde gebraucht und die zerstörten Gebäude wurden wieder aufgebaut. Es war eine Menge Arbeit und es dauerte mehrere Jahre unsere Stadt wieder herzustellen. Geflüchtete Bürger von Ludwigshafen kehrten zurück, aber es gab keinen Platz für sie. Der Bürgermeister versuchte sie davon abzuhalten, weil es nicht möglich war, für sie eine Wohnung zu finden.

Ich beendete die Schule und fand eine Stelle bei der amerikanischen Verwaltung als Büroangestellte. Meine Freundinnen beneideten mich, weil das Gehalt etwas besser als in deutschen Firmen war. Während meiner Arbeit in der amerikanischen Verwaltung lernte ich einen Amerikaner kennen. Es war ein bischen problematisch so kurz nach dem Krieg mit einem amerikanischen Soldaten auszugehen. Die Männer in meinem Büro waren sehr bitter; aber nach längerer Zeit hatten sie sich damit abgefunden.

Es gab so viel in der amerikanischen Zone zu tun. Wir konnten in das amerikanische Kino gehen und in die „Snack Bar" wo ich essen konnte soviel ich wollte. Manches mal marschierten die Amerikaner durch die Straße und man mußte sie bewundern wie sauber und stramm sie aussahen.

Ich wollte meinen Bekannten meinen Eltern vorstellen, aber sogar die Amerikaner mußten einen Paß besitzen um in die französiche Besatzungszone zu gehen. Nach zwei Jahre verlobten wir uns und dann heirateten wir. In 1953 verließ ich meine Heimatstadt um mein Leben in den USA weiterzuführen. Ich werde meinen Abschied von Zuhause nie vergessen. Meine Eltern brachten mich zum Bahnhof; mein Vater war wie ein gebrochener Mann. Er sagte mir daß er mich lieber auf dem Friedhof hätte, damit er mich am Grab besuchen könnte, anstatt daß ich nach Amerika gehe und er mich bestimmt nie wieder sehen wird. Er starb 1955.

Mein Mann und ich, als wir uns kennen lernten

Wenn ich meine Heimatstadt besuche, mache ich öfters eine
Busfahrt mit meiner Freundin. Auf solch einer Fahrt lernte ich eine
Frau kennen und wir kamen ins Gespräch; sie fragte nach meinem
Mädchennamen. Als ich ihr das sagte, hat sie geschrien und war ganz

aufgeregt und ich konnte mir nicht denken warum sie so aufgeregt war. Sie sagte, dass wir zusammen in die Schule gingen und zusammen im KLV Lager waren, wir teilten sogar das gleiche Zimmer. Ich war sprachlos, das war vor 60 Jahren und durch Zufall trafen wir uns wieder. Sie sagte, dass sie öfters an mich dachte und sich wunderte was aus mit geworden war. Sie ist noch in Verbindung mit den anderen Schulkameradinnen und als sie jedem davon erzählte, trafen wir uns und feierten unser Zusammensein bevor ich in die USA zurückflog. Seitdem machen wir jedes Jahr ein Schultreffen wenn ich in Ludwigshafen bin.

Wenn ich in meine Heimatstadt besuche, kann ich sehen, was für Fortschritte gemacht wurden. Ludwigshafen sah oft wie eine riesige Baustelle aus. Von Anfang an wurde dem allgemeinen Bebauungsplan eine überraschende Weitsicht zu Grunde gelegt. Die Stadtväter waren einstimmig der Auffassung, die restlos zerstörte Stadt wieder aufzubauen. Ausgedehnte Parks und Grün füllen die Flächen zwischen den einzelnen Vierteln. Umgehungsstraßen helfen den Stadtkern von allem unnötigem Verkehr frei zu halten.

Ludwigshafen wird natürlich von der Industrie geprägt, die von Anfang an seine Wiege war. Sie ist zusammen mit der Stadt gewachsen. Trotz seiner Industriekomplexe, riesiger Konzerne und weltweiter Chemieunternehmen, ist Ludwigshafen jetzt eine Stadt geworden, in der es wert ist zu leben.

Der neue Bahnhof

Die neue Straße zur Rheinbrücke

Eine neue Einkaufsstraße

Blick auf Ludwigshafen und den Rhein mit Mannheim im Hintergrund

Bismarkstrasse

Ludwigshafen am Rhein bei Nacht

NACHWORT

Ich möchte mit dieser Geschichte zeigen, wie verblendet wir dem Führer folgten, der uns eine herrliche Zukunft für Deutschland versprach. Er ließ sich nicht stoppen andere Länder anzugreifen und dabei Millionen unschuldige Menschen zu töten. Er nahm das beste von Deutschland und richtete es zu Grunde mit seinem übelgesinnten Zweck. Er nahm die Treue der deutschen Leute und führte sie in einen endlosen, hoffnungslosen Krieg. Er nahm die Tapferkeit der Jugend und befahl ihnen zu sterben.

Als ein Mitglied der Hitler Jugend glaubte ich, daß ich ein Teil von etwas ganz besonderem war, das edel und gut und patriotisch war. Als ich von der Nürnberger Prozessen hörte, war ich total verwirrt über unsere deutschen Kriegshelden. Männer wie Admiral Dönitz, Kommandant der U-boote; Erich Räder, Kommandant der Kriegsmarine; Alfred Jodel, Oberhaupt der Wehrmacht und Baldur Von Schirach, unser Jugendführer, sie waren unsere Helden – es war sehr verwirrend. Ich konnte nicht verstehen was diese Männer in meinem Heimatland angerichtet hatten, mit ihren grausamen Handlungen.

Die Verhandlungen waren in Nürnberg zwischen dem 20. November, 1945, und 1. Oktober 1946, für die Hauptkriegsverbrecher. Vierundzwanzig Männer wurden als Kriegsverbrecher angeklagt und wurden vor das Internationale Gericht gebracht. Es bestand aus den vier siegreichen Mächten: Amerika, Großbritannien, Frankreich und Rußland.

Die Verurteilungen wurden am 1. Oktober, 1946 bekanntgegeben. Es war eine tragische Begebenheit. Ich dachte, dass nicht alle zwölf Männer die Todesstrafe verdienten und dass die Freiheitsstrafen sehr hoch waren. Die Welt nannte es „Gerechtigkeit". Der Sieger ist immer der Richter und der Besiegte ist der Angeklagte.

Ich wünschte nur, dass ich damals anderst gedacht hätte, und hätte etwas gegen diese verhängnisvolle Regierung unternommen um Wiederstand zu leisten, aber dazu war ich noch zu jung. Der größte Erfolg aber war, dass ich am Leben blieb und ich danke unserem Herrn Gott daß er immer bei mir war und mich beschützt hat.

1 Wer unter dem Schirm des Höchsten sitzt und unter dem Schatten des Allmächtigen bleibt, 2 der spricht zu dem HERRN: / Meine Zuversicht und meine Burg, mein Gott, auf den ich hoffe. 3 Denn er errettet dich vom Strick des Jägers und von der verderblichen Pest. 4 Er wird dich mit seinen Fittichen decken, und Zuflucht wirst du haben unter seinen Flügeln. Seine Wahrheit ist Schirm und Schild, 5 dass du nicht erschrecken musst vor dem Grauen der Nacht,
(Psalm 91:1-4)

Glücklicherweise habe ich diesen Krieg überlebt und lebe in den USA wo wir frei sind Gott zu verehren und auch die Bibel zu lesen. Während Hitler's Zeit war es uns nicht gestattet im Besitz einer Bibel zu sein oder sie zu lessen. Eine Bekannte gab mir eine Bibel zu Geschenk und seit der Zeit lese ich sie und ich habe Jesus in mein Herz aufgenommen.

Wenn jemand in Christus ist, dann ist er eine neue Schöpfung: *Das Alte ist vergangen, Neues ist geworden.* (*Der zweite Brief an die Korinther 5:17*)

To order additional copies of

THE HITLER I KNEW

Call 888-280-7715

Or please visit our web site at
www.authorhouse.com

Also available at:
www.amazon.com
and
www.google.com

About the Author

Ms. Johnson was born and raised in Ludwigshafen, Germany. After the war and after graduating from Junior College, she went to work for the American Government, where she met her husband who was stationed in Mannheim. She came to the US with her husband in 1953 and became a US citizen. She still has family and friends in Germany, where she visits every year.

Currently she resides in rural Northeast Pennsylvania with her husband. Besides writing and researching history, she also enjoys reading, gardening and doing crafts.